BRENT LIBRARIES

Please return/renew this item
by the last date shown.
Books may also be renewed by
phone or online.
Tel: 0333 370 4700
On-line www.brent.gov.uk/libraryservice

D1334502

DISGUSTING HISTORY

The Horrible, Miserable MIDDLE AGES

THE DISGUSTING DETAILS ABOUT LIFE DURING MEDIEVAL TIMES

by Kathy Allen

raintree

a Capstone company — publishers for children

Raintree is an imprint of Capstone Global Library Limited, a company incorporated in England and Wales having its registered office at 264 Banbury Road, Oxford, OX2 7DY – Registered company number: 6695582

www.raintree.co.uk
myorders@raintree.co.uk

Edited by Christine Peterson
Designed by Alison Thiele
Picture research by Wanda Winch
Production by Eric Manske

ISBN 978 1 4747 1961 2
19 18 17 16 15
10 9 8 7 6 5 4 3 2 1

British Library Cataloguing in Publication Data
A full catalogue record for this book is available from the British Library

Photo Credits
Alamy/The London Art Archi... ...odena/Alfredo Dagli Orti, 10; Art Resource, N.Y./D... ...nan Art Library/Archives Charmet/Private Collection/... ...am Art Gallery & Museums, Gloucestershire, UK/Koedyck... ...ry/Giraudon/Musee des Beaux-Arts, Marseille, France, ... 16; Corbis/Bettmann, 21; Getty Images Inc./The Bridge... ...nger Collection, New York, 9; Mary Evans Picture Library... ...velopment Corporation, 4 (feudal system icons), 5 (churc... ...ook) 9, 29; Shutterstock/ Boris Stroujko, 4 (castle); Shut... ...tist, design element throughout; Shutterstock/Isa... ...r); Shutterstock/Turi Tamas, design element throughout

Primary source bibliography
Page 9 — from *The Excruciatin... ...ties from Babylon to Braces* by James ...

Page 29 — from *The Decameron* by Giovanni Boccaccio as published in *Decameron/Giovanni Boccaccio*, translated from the Italian and introduced by J. G. Nichols (New York: Everyman's Library/ Alfred A. Knopf, 2009).

We would like to thank Phillip C. Adamo for his invaluable help in the preparation of this book.

Printed and bound in China.

CONTENTS

EUROPE DURING THE MIDDLE AGES
AD 476–1400

AD 476 PAGE 6

The last Roman emperor in the West is removed from power. Some historians use this date to mark the beginning of the Middle Ages.

AD 800 PAGE 6

Cities are in decline. Most people live in the country on manors owned by lords.

AD 1000

Armed horseman called knights serve their lords in battle. They become a symbol of the Middle Ages.

MEDIEVAL SOCIAL ORDER
–ALSO CALLED THE FEUDAL SYSTEM–

KING

NOBLES

KNIGHTS

PEASANTS AND SERFS

AROUND AD 800

New farming techniques are invented that allow medieval farmers to grow more food.

PAGE 20 **AROUND AD 1050**

Medieval people start to live in towns for the first time since the Roman Empire collapsed.

LONDON

ROUEN

PARIS

CHURCHES

The church was a major force in people's lives during the Middle Ages. It touched everything from medicine and law to education and government.

ROMAN EMPEROR

After the fall of the Roman Empire, the ruler of Constantinople in modern-day Turkey continued to call himself the "Roman emperor." This "Roman emperor" in the East lasted until 1453.

BLACK SEA

CONSTANTINOPLE

ROME

KEY

⬤ EUROPEAN CITIES

0 ———————— 500 MILES

0 ———————— 500 KILOMETRES

N
W — E
S

THE DANSE MACABRE, OR DANCE OF DEATH

After the plague, many artists focused on the subject of death. They painted images of the Danse Macabre, or Dance of Death. These paintings show nobles and peasants dancing to the music of death.

MEDITERRANEAN SEA

AD 1095

The crusades begin. The crusades were a series of wars between Christians from western Europe and Muslims. These wars would go on for almost 200 years.

PAGE 27

AD 1347

The plague begins to spread through Europe from the Crimea, near the Black Sea. The disease kills about 25 million people over the next four years.

AROUND AD 1400

Some historians mark this time as the end of the Middle Ages and the beginning of the Renaissance.

AD 1200-1225

PAGE 20

The city of Rouen, France, burns to the ground six times.

DIRTY WORK

In AD 476, the fall of the Western Roman Empire gave way to the Middle Ages. Some things in the Middle Ages were great. But other things were filthy!

During this time, Europe was made up of manors, run by lords. **Serfs** were bound to these estates and paid money to the lord of the manor. Serfs worked the fields from dawn to dusk.

Nobles didn't control **peasants**, but that didn't make their lives easier. Peasants farmed the land under a blazing sun and in driving rain. And by the end of the day, they smelt. With no running water, there was no easy way to wash off the filth. Most peasants bathed once a week at most. They bathed in water from nearby streams where they also tipped sewage and rubbish.

The water used for laundry was just as nasty. Peasants wore the same stiff, itchy clothes day in and day out. Some woolen clothing was never washed but simply brushed.

Peasants did what they could to stay clean. They washed their hands several times a day. After meals, they got into pairs with friends and family members to pick off the lice crawling on their clothes.

serf farm worker who was bound to the land and paid money to the lord of the manor

peasant person in Europe who worked on a farm or owned a small farm

Serfs and peasants worked long hours in fields.

ROTTING TEETH

The only things that smelt worse than peasants' clothing in the Middle Ages were their dirty, rotting teeth. People didn't use toothbrushes or toothpaste. Many chewed herbs to cover their smelly breath. They also rinsed with vinegar and wine to clean their mouths.

Bad breath was the least of their dental worries. Treatments for **cavities** and rotten teeth were few. Some people wrongly believed worms caused cavities. They placed an open flame under their jaw to force "worms" out of their gums. Others turned to a tooth-puller, who was often also a barber. These untrained doctors pulled teeth from the gums with a pair of pliers.

Trained doctors would not pull teeth because the patient could die from bleeding. Rich patients who survived this treatment replaced their pulled teeth with false ones made from cow bone. Most people, however, were left gumming their stale bread.

cavity decayed part of a tooth

MEDIEVAL DENTIST

A proven remedy

Take some newts, by some called lizards, and those nasty beetles which are found in fens [marshes] during the summer time, calcine [heat] them in an iron pot and make a powder thereof.

Wet the forefinger of the right hand, insert it in the powder, and apply it to the tooth frequently, refraining from spitting it off, when the tooth will fall away without pain. It is proven.

From a 13th-century guide to curing a toothache (Not to be tried at home!)

Families gutted animals and prepared food in their homes.

TRENCHERS AND OTHER TREATS

Dry bread and a lack of vitamins left commoners with loose teeth and spongy gums. People suffered from **scurvy** and other illnesses because their diet had no variety. Most people filled up on bread, beer and a mushy porridge made from vegetables and grains. Without fridges, fruits and vegetables could not be chilled or transported. People only ate what was in season and available.

Meat was too expensive for most commoners. Peasants ate whatever they could catch, including rabbits, wild beavers and pigeons. Neither peasants nor nobles could afford to let valuable meat spoil. They often dried meat to stop it rotting. Then they boiled it back into chunks that were easy to chew. To make this meat mush taste better, they used many spices. Meat was also preserved in gelatin, made from boiled cows' hooves.

scurvy deadly disease caused by a lack of vitamin C; scurvy produces swollen limbs, bleeding gums and weakness

With so few foods available, nothing could be wasted. Chefs of the nobles served animal brains, lungs and stomachs. The rich feasted on such delights as bear paws, boar guts and other organ meat.

Cooks were creative. Surprise dishes, such as a goose hidden inside a peacock, would delight the nobles and their guests. Also pleasing were meals made of animal pairs. Chefs would serve the front end of a chicken sewn onto the rear end of a piglet.

Meat was sometimes eaten on trenchers. These stale pieces of bread soaked up grease and juices. When the lords had finished eating, they gave the trenchers to peasants. For peasants, these soaked, stale pieces of bread were a real treat!

Nobles feasted on large meals that were often shared with pets. Any leftovers were given to peasants.

FOUL FACT

People in the Middle Ages didn't have toilet paper. Instead, they used lace, wool, hay, leaves and even seashells.

MEDIEVAL CASTLE TOILET

NO FLUSHING

The food in the Middle Ages left many doubled over and running for the nearest lavatory. It's a good thing many homes had indoor toilets. But people didn't want to spend a lot of time in medieval loos. Waste wasn't flushed away. Instead, a simple wooden toilet connected to a small pipe. The pipe carried the waste away, but not too far. The waste pooled in a hole behind the house called a cesspit. This pit was lined with wood or stone so it wouldn't leak to other areas.

In England, the men who cleaned out cesspits were called gong farmers. These workers filled tubs with waste and emptied them further from town. Gong farmers were hardworking, unpopular people. Covered with smelly waste, they lived only with each other. Some died from breathing the fumes – or worse, falling into the pits.

Townspeople without indoor toilets used outhouses or chamber-pots. An outhouse was basically a shed with a bench. A hole in the bench led to a sewage pit below. Those without an outhouse used chamber-pots. They sometimes emptied these pots out of the window, onto the street below. This practice wasn't common, as people could be fined for adding to the town's filth.

Some people built their homes above a stream, so their toilet could empty into it. People often said "bridges are for wise men to go over, and fools to go under". Fools also used public toilets. These dirty loos had wooden floors and weren't always safe. Records show that some people fell through toilet floors, into the filth below. The clever ones knew to hold on until they got home.

CHAMBER-POT

FOUL FACT

John the Fearless had a padded toilet seat. The Duke's poos dropped into a stone pit. People can still see it today – the pit that is, not the poo.

COLD CASTLES

Nobles lived in huge, stone castles or large manor houses. While the homes looked beautiful from the outside, inside they could be cold and dark.

Fireplaces were the main source of heat for castles. But this warmth was usually reserved for the lord and his family, especially at night. Servants and workers sometimes slept on cold, stone floors. Their only heat came from kitchen fires.

Toilets in castles often had no windows to let out the smell of human waste. Toilets were sometimes built sticking out from the walls of castle towers. Waste from these bathrooms fell on whatever – or whomever – happened to be below.

Most castles were built as military sites and often came under attack. Capturing a castle wasn't an easy task. Attackers often waded through wide moats filled with dirty water, underwater spikes and human and animal waste. Others crawled through filthy toilet shafts to enter the building!

Medieval castles looked beautiful, but they were cold, smelly places.

MEDIEVAL TOWNS

By AD 1050, rows of small houses cropped up in towns across Europe. Peasants often lived in cramped one-room houses. Animals, including cows, would often share the same room with family members.

Later houses had two floors. They had a shop on the groundfloor and living space above. Homes were built close together and often made from wood and straw. Indoor fires cooked food and provided heat, but they also burnt people and houses. The French city of Rouen burnt down six times in 25 years.

If things were somewhat smelly inside homes, they were even worse on city streets. Animals were often gutted at market. Their innards were thrown onto the street. Blood and guts flowed through a gutter in the middle of streets made of hard-packed dirt. Wider streets had gutters on both sides to collect animal waste. Men called rakers piled rubbsh into carts and dumped it downwind of town.

Medieval towns were filled with shops, waste and smells.

People were fined for polluting the town with animal guts. Towns also tried to stop the smelly practice of selling spoilt meat. Anyone caught selling rotten food would have their goods burnt as punishment. They were also forced to sit very close to the fire, breathing the smell of burning spoilt meat. It's no wonder people held flowers on their way through town to combat the smell of everyday life.

BARBER-SURGEONS

From town to country, people in medieval times led lives marked by illness and injury. Hard work, animal bites and battle wounds left many in need of doctors. There were medical schools, but few doctors to be found. Only the rich could afford a trained doctor. Even these professionals sometimes used odd medicines, such as ground-up earthworms.

Those who could not afford doctors relied on folk medicine and common healers to cure them. Patients swallowed herbs or chanted to cure sickness. At best, these folk cures did no harm. At worst, they killed the patient. Some treatments were more gross than deadly, such as putting pig poo on a bleeding nose. Some animal dung treatments actually worked, but you won't find them used in a doctor's surgery today.

Few medieval doctors had formal training. Many tried peculiar treatments to cure patients.

For bigger health problems, those who could not find a doctor went to the next best thing: a barber-surgeon. Barber-surgeons performed a common operation called **bloodletting**. The same knives and razors used for haircuts came in handy for this treatment. For this operation, a barber made a small cut in the vein of a patient and let the blood pool in a dish. The barber then studied the blood for clues as to what was making the person sick. Barbers studied blood by smelling it, touching it and even tasting it. Barber-surgeons also tested urine by tasting it.

Most surgeries of the time were simple. The most serious operations were for those wounded in battle. Even for amputations, surgeons didn't have very good medicines. Lucky patients would pass out at the first cut of a crude saw. Other patients breathed chemicals on a soaked rag, which could also kill them.

MEDIEVAL BLOODLETTING KNIFE

bloodletting practice of removing blood by opening a vein

People believed that bloodletting would rid them of disease.

FOUL FACT

Medieval doctors also used leeches to suck blood from patients. Some doctors still use leeches today!

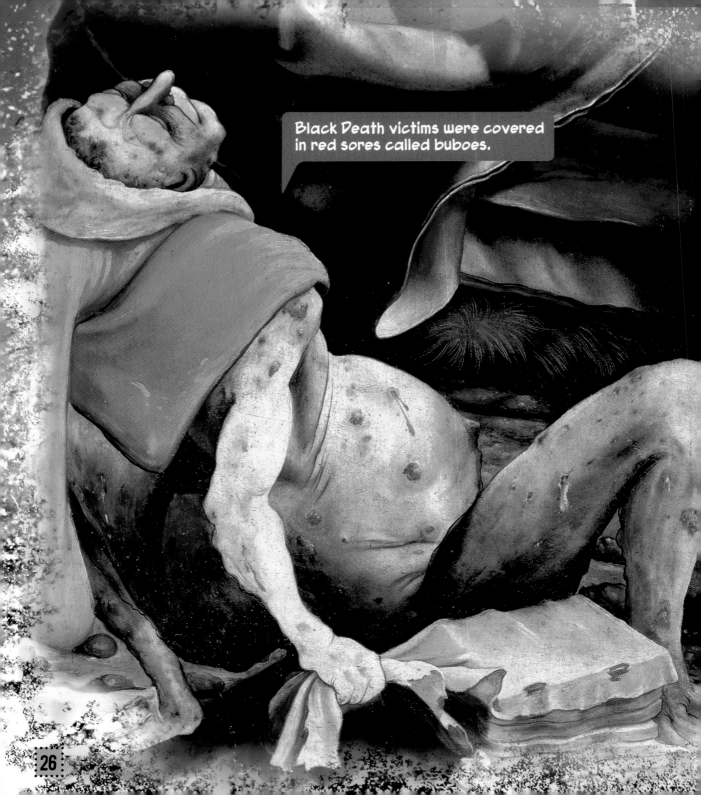

PLAGUE HORRORS

Doctors and barber-surgeons were not ready for the **plague** that swept through Europe in the mid-1300s. The plague, called Black Death, killed nearly one-third of the people in Europe. People caught the plague from fleas that had feasted on wild rats. Once the plague took hold, it could kill within a week. Panic swept through towns and villages. Even doctors ran in fear from patients with signs of the plague.

The first symptom was usually a small, black bump where a diseased flea had bitten the person. Larger bumps, called buboes, soon followed. Buboes were often found in the neck, armpits or groin area. These bumps could be as small as an egg or as large as an apple. Next, dark spots of blood seeping beneath the skin spread throughout the body. By this time, little could be done to save the patient. The total number of dead was too many for even the biggest towns to handle.

plague serious disease that spreads quickly and often causes death

Bodies were left outside homes to be picked up by passing workers. These workers were often released prisoners. They were the only ones willing to do the dirty job of collecting dead bodies. Mass graves filled quickly. Some bodies were dumped into the sea. Other bodies were left to lie in the street.

Adding to the horror were patients gone mad with disease and fright. Some would dance on the rooftops, while others dug their own graves. Leaving piles of dead, the plague was a most disgusting time in the Middle Ages.

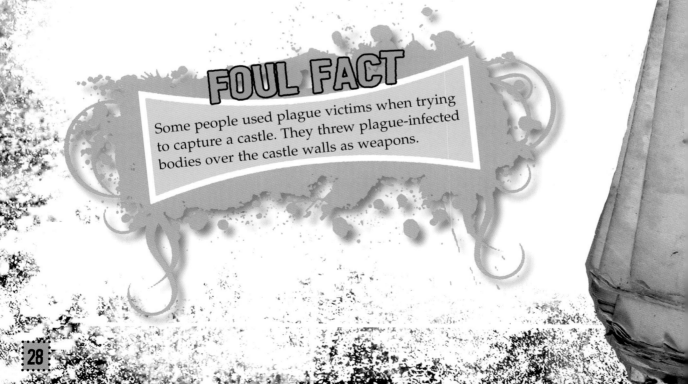

FOUL FACT

Some people used plague victims when trying to capture a castle. They threw plague-infected bodies over the castle walls as weapons.

A pitiful sight

In a book called The Decameron, written in the 1350s, Giovanni Boccaccio describes the disgusting sights and smells of the plague:

The plight of the lower and most of the middle classes was even more pitiful to behold. Most of them remained in their houses, either through poverty or in hopes of safety, and fell sick by thousands. Since they received no care and attention, almost all of them died. Many ended their lives in the streets both at night and during the day; and many others who died in their houses were only known to be dead because the neighbours smelt their decaying bodies. Dead bodies filled every corner.

GLOSSARY

bloodletting practice of removing blood by opening a vein

cavity decayed part of a tooth

peasant person in Europe who worked on a farm or owned a small farm

plague very serious disease that spreads quickly to many people and often causes death

scurvy deadly disease caused by lack of vitamin C; scurvy produces swollen limbs, bleeding gums and weakness

serf farm worker who was bound to the land and paid money to the lord of the manor

READ MORE

Life in Medieval Britain (A Child's History of Britain), Anita Ganeri (Raintree, 2014)

Medieval Knights (Fierce Fighters), Charlotte Guillain (Raintree, 2012)

The Middle Ages (History of Britain), Abigail Wheatley (Usborne Publishing Ltd, 2015)

WEBSITES

www.bbc.co.uk/history/british/middle_ages
Learn about kings, conflicts and plagues during the Middle Ages.

www.kidsdiscover.com/spotlight/castles-for-kids
Take a look at pictures and discover facts about medieval castles.

INDEX